D1297036

WILD ANIMALS

GALLERY BOOKS
An Imprint of W. H. Smith Publishers Inc.
112 Madison Avenue
New York City 10016

This edition first published in U.S.
in 1990 by Gallery Books,
an imprint of W.H. Smith Publishers, Inc.
112 Madison Avenue, New York, New York 10016

ISBN 0-8317-9589-1

Printed and bound in Spain

For rights information about the photographs in
this book please contact:

The Image Bank
111 Fifth Avenue, New York, NY 10003

Producer: Solomon M. Skolnick
Author: Marcus Schneck
Design Concept: Lesley Ehlers
Designer: Ann-Louise Lipman
Editor: Terri L. Hardin
Production: Valerie Zars
Photo Researcher: Edward Douglas
Assistant Photo Researcher: Robert Hale

Title page: **Probably no animal symbolizes Africa more than the male lion, often called "The King of Beasts." In reality, the big cat is a rather lazy creature, generally relying on the lionesses of his pride to make the kills.** *Opposite:* **Elephants are the largest land mammals. Their huge ivory tusks continue to attract poachers despite a growing international ban on all products made of ivory.**

"**W**ild" is defined by the American Heritage Dictionary of the English Language (New College Edition) as having four meanings. The first is "occurring, growing, or living in a natural state; not domesticated, cultivated or tamed." The second meaning is "not inhabited; desolate," the third is "uncivilized or barbarous; savage," and the fourth is "lacking discipline, restraint, or control; unruly." And while the first definition properly applies to the subject of this book, it often happens that wild animals are judged by the others. For example, an area without human inhabitants is often regarded as "uninhabited," no matter how many other types of inhabitants are within. An area undeveloped by modern standards is "uncivilized," and any animals that do not conform to human desires are certainly seen as "unruly."

Examples of human discomfort in and distrust of the wild are manifold. At the Gouin Reservoir in central Quebec, the night often has a darkness to it that just isn't to be found near cities, or towns, or any of man's settlements where artificial lighting illuminates the crisp black sky. There, where dancing

Elephant herds, for much of the year, are made up of matriarch-dominated, extended family groups.

To maintain their massive bodies, elephants spend the vast majority of their waking hours engaged in eating. They will travel extensively to satisfy this need for food, sometimes as far as 40 miles in a single night. *Opposite:* Hippopotami spend most of their days in the water, living up to the Greek origin of their name, "river horse." At night hippos leave their daytime aquatic sanctuaries to roam for miles on land in search of suitable grazing sites. Each adult may eat as much as 200 pounds of grass in a night.

Preceding page: The rare black rhino is a solitary creature, often spending most of its life alone. *This page:* White rhinos (top) travel in family groups that can include a half dozen individuals. Pressures of land development in overcrowded Asian countries, along with the inherent dangers of inbreeding, have placed the one-horned Indian rhinoceros in severe jeopardy (bottom).

Preceding page: This female giraffe has three times the normal amount of care to give, with an extremely rare set of triplets. *This page:* The giraffe's long tongue enables the animal to extend its 17-foot height advantage even further above competing plant-eaters, to reach vegetation they have no hope of eating. *Overleaf:* To survive the predations of the large meat-eaters, the impala has evolved leg muscling that enables it to jump 35 feet in a single bound.

Some antelope species, such as the impala, graze on grass during the wet season, switching to a diet of bark and buds in the dry season.

columns of light – the Aurora Borealis – flash across the star-filled heavens, the pale yellow glow of a gas lantern, filtered through the screens of a cabin's windows, can be the brightest spot on the horizon.

It was there, somewhere in the dense northern forest across the lake, that a wolf once howled and then howled again. A few seconds passed and then a second wolf answered the call of the first, this one much closer and on the near side of the water.

Neither wolf posed any real threat to the human occupants vacationing in the cabin along the shoreline, isolated as it was from the nearest cabin (miles away) and an hour's plane ride away from civilization. The wild canines were much further off than their long-carrying calls seemed to place them. They had no intention, no reason, to come any closer to the foreign human creatures.

And yet, their spine-tingling cries raised the hairs on the back of my neck.

Top to bottom: Grant's gazelle males are extremely territorial, sometimes defending their areas even after the females have moved on. The New York Zoological Society's Rare Animal Survival Center on St. Catherine's Island (off the coast of Georgia) has helped the endangered slender-horned gazelle to stage something of a small comeback. Thomson's gazelles are the most numerous animals of the African plains herds.

These wolves were wild creatures in every sense of the word. This was their land. They roamed it on their own terms. There was a very good chance that they had never seen a human and perhaps never would.

The wolf is one of those creatures that so neatly defines the word "wild" for us humans. Even when all the myth, folklore and misconception has been stripped away, it stands as cause for thoughts of things beyond our normal, everyday lives. Wolves, and animals like them, are the last remnants of what the entire earth once was, reminders that bits of that former world persist, often in spite of our best efforts to the contrary.

In today's world, wild is all too scarce, something that must be sought out and, if found, cherished. Those animals that still have wilderness in them capture the imagination. They may even be cause for envy.

Preceding pages: Wildebeest travel in herds numbering more than 100,000 head. Their range extends from the southern portion of Africa's Serengeti Plain to the abundant food and water of the northwest at the start of each year's dry season. *This page, top to bottom:* The water buffalo fears few other animals, and has been known to attack a tiger in order to drive the big cat away from the herd. Hunters prize the water buffalo as a trophy, partly because of its dangerous reputation. To save the musk ox from extinction, several wild individuals have been taken into domestication.

Wild and consequently free (although those descriptions have no meaning to them), wild animals do nothing more, nothing less, each and every day than follow the habits and routines that their line has followed for generations. Adequate food and water, protection from enemies, and the opportunity to rear the next generation are their motivations. Being wild and free is simply the means that the animals have employed to accomplish these goals.

After the cheetah, the pronghorn is the fastest land animal on earth. Unlike true antelopes, the pronghorn sheds the sheath of its horns annually. *Below:* The zebra is a prime example of disruptive coloration in the animal kingdom; the striped pattern breaks the wild equine's outline, making it less noticeable to predators.

Preceding page: Wood Buffalo National Park in northwest Canada was created in 1922 to protect the wood bison, a darker, larger subspecies of the North American bison. *This page:* Estimates have placed the number of bison (top) at more than 60 million across the North American continent before the arrival of the "white man." From the age of three to about 30 years, a female bison (below)—under prime feeding conditions—can bear one calf each year.

Such things as brown bear tracks across a trail through Alaska's Arctic National Wildlife Refuge, or a bull moose nibbling its way through a mountain meadow in Yellowstone National Park, remind us that there are still places in the world where we are not always alone at the very peak of the chain of life. There are still animals that have not accepted us as their rulers.

But wild is not only to be found in the wilderness. The white-tailed deer that's currently enjoying a population boom across most of the United States is quickly becoming a resident of the suburbs as well as the forest, but it remains wild. Even the gray squirrel that raids the backyard bird feeder every morning remains a wild creature, following the same natural lifestyle as has its species for hundreds of generations.

Nor is wild anywhere near the exclusive province of North America. Although there might be better access to it in North America than much of the rest of the world, there are much greater wild places elsewhere. In spite of humanity's ever-tightening stranglehold on the earth and its resources, wild animals continue to exist across the globe, holding out the hope that not everything must be civilized and tamed.

Preceding page: Herds of barren ground caribou may cover as much as 600 miles one-way during their annual spring and fall migrations. *This page:* The moose (top) can weigh as much as 2,000 pounds, and spend its entire life within a 10-mile home range. In the fall rutting season, bull elk (bottom) spend nearly all their time and energies in collecting and maintaining harems of cows for breeding.

This page: The mule deer (top) ranges throughout the western states and provinces, where it is the most important big-game animal. Mule deer does (bottom) bear one to three fawns each May to June after the age of two.

The white-tailed deer, while heavily hunted, has also prospered and extended its range in the shadow of civilization. Suburban herds are beginning to cause problems in the eastern United States.

Elephants and rhinos still roam the thornbush country of Africa, the last of the many giant creatures that once ranged throughout the world. Some of their population is now maintained only under very close protection, as poachers have pursued them relentlessly for their ivory tusks and horns.

In the grasslands of that same continent, the largest remaining wild herds of animals follow the same annual migration routes carved by their ancestors. Thomson's and Grant's gazelles, wildebeest, and zebras by the thousands push their way back and forth with the changing of the wet and dry seasons.

The greatest herds that the world has ever known, however, were the bison that once roamed the plains of North America. "For six days we continued our way through this enormous herd, during the last three of which it was in constant motion across our path...it is impossible to approximate the millions that composed it. At times they pressed before us in such numbers as to delay the progress of our column," wrote a U.S. Army officer of one

Top to bottom: **Flying squirrels are much more common than generally thought, a fact that is successfully hidden by the animals' highly nocturnal nature. The Columbian ground squirrel hibernates as much as eight months out of every year, entering its sleeping chamber as early as July. The red squirrel, a denizen of the coniferous forest, is a fierce defender of its home range against other squirrels, often driving off the much larger gray squirrel.**

herd he encountered in October 1871. At the time the bison population was already in decline, estimated to still stand at about 15 million head.

Just 16 years later when that same officer, George S. Anderson, became superintendent of Yellowstone National Park, only a few more than 500 of the magnificent, shaggy beasts survived south of the Canadian border. Hunters were in search of meat at first, but later only the hides and tongues of the half-ton animals. Bison had been pushed to the brink of extinction.

Snowshoe hares take on a white coat for the winter months—an important defense against predators. *Below:* The black-tailed jack rabbit can reach speeds of 35 miles per hour over short distances and can leap spans of more than 20 feet.

Fortunately, what could have been the final years on earth for the entire species were also the beginning years of the growing conservation movement. The bison was among the earliest beneficiaries of the changing attitudes. Today the bison population stands at more than 25,000 head, although many do not live under what can truly be described as "wild" conditions.

Although the beaver's ponds may flood timber and crop lands, they create a favorable habitat for a wide range of animal species. *Below:* Caught away from its burrow, the badger may dig one at a fast pace and toss the excavated dirt into the attacker's face.

The hoary marmot makes a shrill alarm whistle similar to the whistle of a man; this has given it the nickname of "whistler." *Below:* Raccoons *do not* insist upon washing food before eating; the myth arose from the animal's habit of probing and grabbing for edibles, like crayfish, among shallow stream beds.

The human being is too efficient a predator. As it was with the bison, a natural system that has functioned for thousands of years near balance can be – in less than a person's lifetime – drastically changed, often bringing the destruction of the creatures that make up the system.

In a naturally functioning, wild system that has been undisturbed, there are the prey species and there are the predators. To the bison there was the wolf, following the herds alone or in packs, picking off the sick, aged and young. To the African herds, there were (and are still) the members of the great cat family, Panthera. Lions, leopards and the like drawn their sustenance by preying upon the herds.

Lesser, or red, pandas live in small groups in the bamboo forests of mountainous China and Tibet. The bamboo is their sole dietary item. *Below:* While efforts are being made to save the giant panda from extinction, a major stumbling-block is habitat reduction. *Opposite:* Commonly referred to as the "panda bear" but thought by some to be more closely related to the raccoon, the giant panda is now classified taxonomically as neither.

This daily struggle to make some other animal into food or to avoid becoming food for some other animal may seem harsh, but it is the way of the wild. Every wild creature functions within such a system. Only people and those animals that have been removed from their natural environments have ceased to follow the rules.

Left to themselves, the systems function to remain relatively balanced. Plant-eaters rise and fall in number in direct relationship to their food supply. Predators also maintain a check on rising plant-eater populations. In turn, the plant-eaters act as a check on the predator population.

The hairs of the polar bear's fur are hollow, providing effective insulation and extra buoyancy in the water. *Opposite:* Polar bears are inhabitants of the far north, well-adapted for life on the Arctic ice and excellent long-distance swimmers.

But human dwellings now occupy so much of what was previously habitat for wildlife that fewer and fewer systems continue to function completely in this manner, and this has had a profound impact. Human enterprises, such as the ongoing destruction of the earth's rain forests, also take a severe toll. Even those creatures that humans choose, such as the dog and cat, throw the system out of balance when they are permitted to act as predators.

When humanity moves in, important parts of "wild" move out. The largest animals – those that often seem to most epitomiz our concept of wild – have generally been the first components of the natural system to go. Competition with – or worse, threatening – humanity has not worked in any animal's favor for thousands of years.

On Australia, the continent "down under," kangaroos were unceremoniously slaughtered when natural resources were needed to support the sheep

Top to bottom: **Fishing techniques of the brown bear vary widely among individual bruins, from simply standing quietly in the current until a spawning salmon swims by to positioning themselves at the exact spot where the fish leap upstream over obstructions. The time of summer plenty is relatively short and the brown bear mus build up as much as an extra 400 pounds of fat in order to get through the long winter. Black bears are becoming increasingly plentiful across North America, as they adapt to life in the shadow of civilization.**

herding industry. Then, in the late 1950's, a market for kangaroo meat as both pet and human food was found, and death and destruction escalated. At one point, about one million kangaroos were killed annually. But the general extinctions that were feared have not come to pass, and the kangaroo seems to be holding on.

For many years the grizzly bear was considered a separate, much more ferocious species, from the brown bear; the two are the same animal, fitted with different man-made names. *Right:* On its own terms, in its own environment, the brown bear is a force to be reckoned with. Tales of attacks on humans, however, are generally exaggerated; more often than not, they are provoked by the human.

Preceding page: Kangaroos can bound along at speeds of 40 miles per hour over short distances, and can leap 27 feet. *This page:* There are dozens of kangaroo species, ranging from the eight-foot-long great red kangaroo (top) to the 16-inch-long rat kangaroo. *Below:* Called "mobs," groups of kangaroos (bottom) traveling together can range to several hundred animals. Dangers are signaled to one another with a thump on the ground with a hind foot.

Koalas spend their entire lives in eucalyptus trees, where they find the leaves that make up their very restrictive diets. *Below:* Baby koalas are weaned from mother's milk by eating half-digested eucalyptus leaves that have passed through the female's digestive tract. *Opposite:* Fur hunters pushed the koala to the edge of extinction in the early 1900's, exporting hundreds of thousands of pelts per year. Today the species is recovering with conservation efforts.

Each fall during the rutting season, bighorn sheep rams engage in head-butting contests, ramming their heads together at speeds of more than 20 miles per hour. *Opposite:* Mountain goat hooves are well designed for rugged mountain life, having sharp, gripping, outer edges and rubbery inner soles.

To survive, wild animals do various things. The white-tailed deer and coyote have adapted, even proliferated, in the growing shadow of civilization. Others, like the grizzly bear and Bengal tiger, have retreated further and further into the remaining wild places. But, whether these animals remain close or remote, they continue in the wild ways that have been programed into them over generations.

In other areas of the world, bears, big cats and wolves were generally the first to be driven from an area at the approach of humanity. Extensive killing of the "offending" animal was generally the first step.

Dall sheep inhabit the rocky, mountainous areas of Alaska and northwest Canada. *Below:* Unfortunately for the greater kudu of Africa, their meat is prized by native hunters and the horns are coveted for the making of musical instruments. *Opposite:* The coyote is a species on the rise, claiming the niche and territory throughout the eastern portion of North America previously occupied by the wolf.

The brown bear, commonly known in America by its more vicious name of grizzly bear, has been persecuted almost off the continent. While there remain stronghold pockets in northern and northwest Canada and Alaska, settlement and development have pushed all but a few hundred of the great bear out of the animal's former range that had extended throughout the North American West. Most are now found only on protected government lands.

Populations of the Arctic fox reach a peak every four years, following the cycle of the lemmings, which are its chief food source. *Below:* The red fox is highly omnivorous, eating a wide variety of vegetation when it's available but turning primarily to small rodents in the winter.

The timber, or gray, wolf maintains regular rendezvous areas within its home range, where the pack gathers when it is not using the den. The area is usually a grassy spot with plenty of rodents. *Right:* Hybridization through breeding with the coyote may doom the red wolf to extinction, the final blow after a long persecution. *Overleaf:* The timber wolf uses a wide range of howls, growls, yelps and barks to communicate with others of its species.

In Europe, where populations of the same bear have been hunted for many more generations, they have adapted their ways to hide themselves and their activities from man and, as a result, have increased in numbers. It has been speculated that this same adaptation to man is taking place among the remaining bears of the lower 48 states. But that raises the question of whether these bears will then be "grizzly bears" in any sense other than carrying the name.

One wonders if that new bear will still carry that wild thrill that John James Audubon described in his book, *The Quadrupeds of North America:*

"Our readers must therefore imagine the startling sensations experienced on a sudden and quite unexpected face-to-face meeting with the savage Grizzly Bear – the huge shaggy monster disputing possession of the wilderness against all comers, and threatening immediate attack!"

Preceding page: Leopards spend a great deal of time in trees, even dragging freshly killed prey up into the branches to protect it from hyenas and jackals. *This page, top to bottom:* The most common wild cat in North America, the bobcat's shy and elusive nature generally conceals its activities from human discovery. Fur hunting and trapping has had a disastrous impact on the ocelot, which has a much sought-after coat. The lynx preys chiefly on the snowshoe hare and consequently follows the same peak-crash, 10-year cycle as that animal.

The bloodcurdling cry of the mountain lion has been described as the scream of a woman both terrified and in pain. *Opposite:* The jaguarundi roams the dense forests of Central and South America, but much of its life cycle has yet to be discovered.

In some protected park areas of eastern Africa, the leopard population is on the rise. It's even becoming possible to view the animal from vehicles during the day. *Below:* Tigers are water-lovers and strong swimmers. *Opposite:* The cheetah show strong preference for fresh meat that they have killed themselves. Vary rarely will they eat carrion, even the leftovers from their own kills.

Audubon showed no such fear for the black bear, the much smaller cousin of the brown. "Such assaults are, however, exceedingly rare, and it is seldom that even a wounded bear attacks man," he wrote.

That was in the 1840's, and already much of the fight had been purged from the animal. Some researchers today believe that the black bear was not always the shy, retiring, noncombative animal it is now. Hundreds of years of man's killing of any black bear that posed even the slightest threat has removed the genetic traits of more threatening bears from the pool.

The bear remains an exceedingly wild creature, although it eagerly adapts to hand-outs and garbage. And, with the traits for danger mostly removed, the bear has enjoyed a tremendous resurgence in total numbers and range throughout much of the United States.

Like the bear, the mountain lion was driven from its native haunts early in the settlement of America. Totally a meat-eater, the big cat simply posed a threat to people and their domesticated animals that they were not prepared to accept.

Once widespread across North America, the mountain lion today roams in scattered pockets of the West. A tiny, dwindling population of a subspecies, the Florida panther, struggles to maintain its final clawhold on a bit of the Everglades.

Reports of the cat also have been mounting throughout its former range east of the Mississippi River, raising hopes that the cougar may still inhabit areas that previously were assumed to be too "tame." Wildlife agencies persist in a no-chance attitude toward all of these sightings, even those made by experienced wildlife researchers and outdoorsmen. But even the chance that the mountain lion still roams there makes a place like, say north central Pennsylvania, just that much wilder.

And, of course, not all has been bleak for the large wild animals of the eastern United States. With the wolf extirpated from its former range, another wild canine has gradually moved in over the past few decades.

A large adult lion may eat 75 pounds of meat in a single day, when hunting is good. *Below:* The lionesses do most of the hunting and other work of the pride. *Opposite:* Lions may sleep as much as 20 hours every day, rising only to hunt in the early morning or evening, if undisturbed.

Some estimates place the entire snow leopard population at only 500 animals. The big cat is a victim of its magnificent fur, among the most valuable on the illegal fur market. *Opposite:* Gibbons rush through the treetops of their forest homes in sweeping, acrobatic motions known as brachiating.

Orangutan in Malaysian means "old man of the forest"; unfortunately, forests on Sumatra and Borneo are disappearing at an astonishing rate. *Below:* Baboons live in troops of as many as 100 animals, dominated by a single male or a cooperating group of males. *Opposite:* Orangutans spend their nights on individual platforms that they construct of branches and leaves in the forks of trees.

The coyote is much better adapted to life near civilization than the larger wolf. While maintaining its wildness, the coyote has learned to take advantage of every opportunity presented to it, from herds of sheep to garbage cans to the rodents that proliferate at garbage dumps.

While coyote attacks have been reported and the animal always presents the possibility of rabies, the canine presents no direct threat to people. The threat to livestock is much more real and severe, leading to many attempts to eradicate the coyote and calls for even more. However, the coyote as a wild species is in no danger whatsoever of disappearing. Every attempt to do away with the animal has simply served to kill some individuals, while causing the female coyotes to compensate biologically with larger numbers of offspring, and the overall increase to the population and range.

Relatively few animals have the resilience of the coyote, and in particular, very few of the larger animals. The lion, nearly everybody's image of the wild creature, is likewise symbolic of the plight of nearly all of Africa's and Asia's big cats. Gradually it has been driven from a range that, within historic times, extended

Chimpanzees are among the very few wild animals that modify natural objects to use them as tools, such as a twig stripped of its leaves and used to pull termites from their holes. *Left:* The red howler monkey is a resident of South America's rain forests.

north into Europe and east into the Near East to Africa south of the Sahara Desert.

Sport-hunting has taken its toll on the cats, but the trade in furs such as the magnificent coats of the snow leopard, tiger and cheetah, and constant habitat destruction have been and are the true threats that may hold the final blow for these animals.

Nor has our closest link to the wild – the great apes – escaped the onslaught of *Homo sapiens.* Gorillas have been killed for their heads and paws. Chimpanzees have been shipped by the tens of thousands for pet and research purposes; the traditional method of capture being to kill the mother and take the baby. And orangutans probably have no future outside of captivity, for their native forests in Sumatra and Borneo may not exist much longer.

Although regularly portrayed as a ferocious beast, most of the chest-pounding bravado of the lowland gorilla is nothing more than communicative demonstration. *Below:* **The silverback male is the leader and, when necessary, defender of the gorilla band.**

As bleak as much of this may sound for the continued existence of wild animals on earth, it is not a situation beyond return. Although some of the diversity with which our "Ark" was originally supplied has been lost, every animal described in this book still exists, probably in large enough numbers to give the species at least a limited comeback if conditions are just right. And public attitudes appear to be leaning towards fulfilling those conditions.

The howl of the wolf on a dark, Canadian night not only reminds us of an earlier time, when our own species was much closer to wildness than it is now, it reminds us that our way is not the only means of survival. For these reasons, and many others, wild animals are entirely deserving of our respect and consideration.

Spider monkeys have long, fully prehensile tails which they use in climbing and to hold food items. *Below:* Troops of douc langurs make a great deal of fuss over their infants. *Opposite:* The leaf monkey lives in the wintery, coniferous forests of the high Himalayan Mountains, well adapted to the cold, snowy climate.

Index of Photography